HEART
OF THE
FAMILY CIRCUS

FAWCETT COLUMBINE • NEW YORK

A Fawcett Columbine Book
Published by Ballantine Books

Copyright © 1986 by Cowles Syndicate, Inc.
THE FAMILY CIRCUS® copyright © 1981, 1982, 1983, 1984 by
the Register and Tribune Syndicate, Inc.

Library of Congress Catalog Card Number: 85-90896

ISBN: 0-449-90148-3

Manufactured in the United States of America

Designed by Gene Siegel

First Edition: May 1986

10   9   8   7   6   5   4   3   2   1

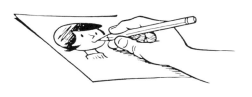

WHILE SHE DOESN'T GET TO SPEAK THE FUNNY LINES IN MY CARTOONS, MOMMY IS THE MOST IMPORTANT CHARACTER I DRAW.

HER PATIENT, UNDERSTANDING ATTITUDE SETS THE STAGE AND THE MOOD FOR MOST OF THE IDEAS. THESE PORTRAYALS OF TYPICAL CHILDHOOD SCENES WORK LARGELY BECAUSE READERS KNOW MOMMY IS ALWAYS DEPENDABLY THERE -- WHETHER SHE IS SHOWN OR NOT.

IN ADDITION TO BEING BEAUTIFUL SHE IS MANY THINGS:

 COUNSELOR, DISCIPLINARIAN, PHILOSOPHER,

DECISION MAKER, LOVER, -- THE HEART OF THE FAMILY CIRCUS!

BIL KEANE

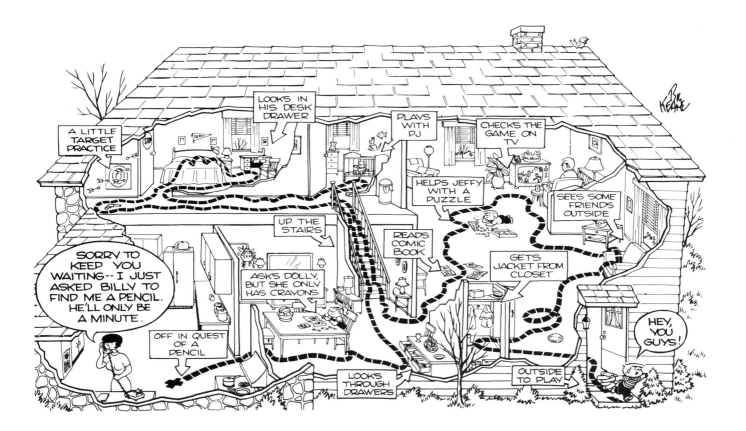

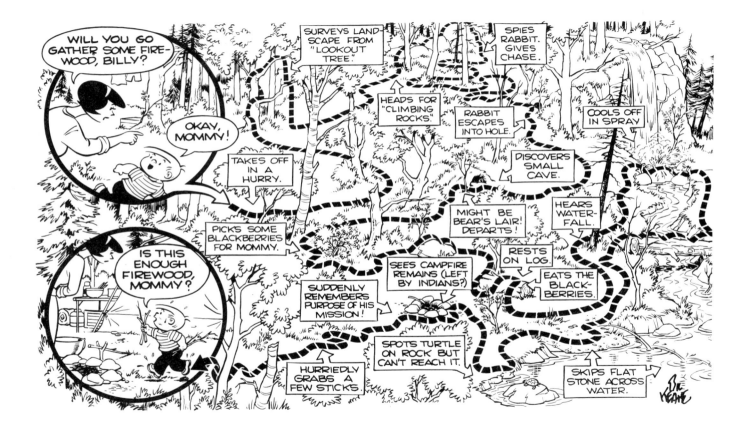

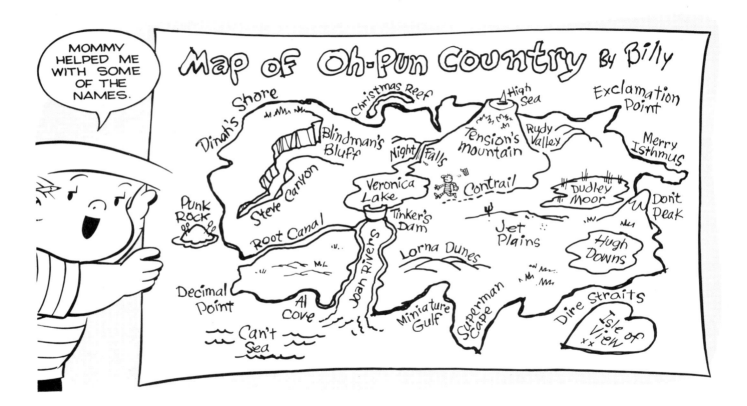

GOOD MORNING SUNSHINE!

When Daddy takes us Trick or Treating we make him hide so the neighbors won't ~~reekinise~~ ~~recanize~~ know it's us.

Mommy usually stays home and answers the door. She says Daddy has the best deal.

Jeffy never wants to wear what I wore last year.

Some kids just have a party at home instead of going around to houses because there are some really wierd people in this world!

Second best part of Halloween is counting the loot.

Best part is eating it!

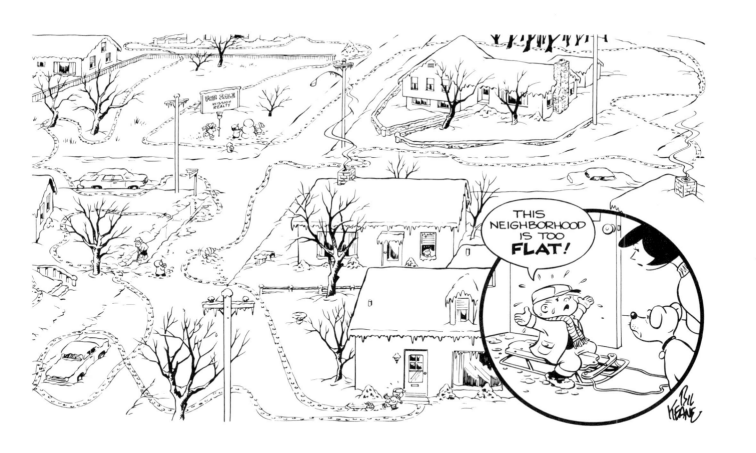

REAL LIFE NURSERY RHYMES

RUB-A-DUB-DUB THREE MEN IN A TUB

GO ASK YOUR MOTHER FOR FIFTY CENTS

SIMPLE SIMON MET A PIEMAN

LUCY LOCKET LOST HER POCKET

RAIN, RAIN, GO AWAY!

LITTLE BILLY FILLS IN FOR THE VACATIONING BIL KEANE

What If...

By Billy

What if Humpty Dumpty had been hard-boiled?

The old woman in the shoe lived in an Adults-Only Development?

Margery Daw liked to play on a trampoline?

What if Old King Cole was grumpy?

Jack and Jill had lived on the plains?

What if Little Miss Muffet had sprayed her place with "Spider-Ded"?

Peter Piper had picked a peck of fried zucchini?

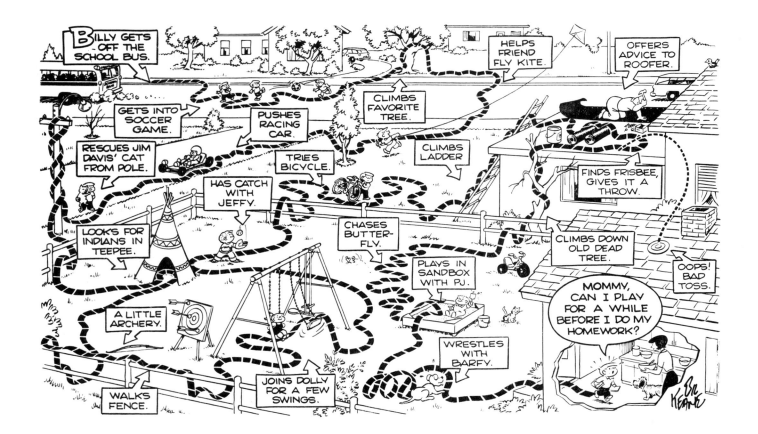

WAKE UP, DADDY! IT'S SNOWIN'!
APRIL 1
APRIL FOOL!
COME LOOK, DADDY! I'LL SHOW YOU!
SNOW? WOW! I'LL HAVE TO GO LOOK! WE CAN BUILD A NICE SNOWMAN!
THEN WE CAN GO SLEDDING! AND THROW SNOWBALLS...
LET'S GO SEE ALL THIS SNOW.
CAN WE START WITH THE SNOWMAN NOW?
BIL KEANE

A Personal Reflection
By Bil Keane

The model for Mommy in these cartoons is my wife Thel. I met the former Thelma Carne in Australia where I was stationed as a member of the U.S. Army during World War II. The war ended and I returned to my home in Philadelphia, Pa. I wrote many letters to my wartime girlfriend, but to no avail. Her logical conclusion was that we were 10,000 miles apart, from different countries, both with our own friends. Why try to perpetuate a fleeting relationship?

But I wouldn't take no for an answer. I drew cartoons in my letters depicting myself as a forlorn guy with a broken heart hovering over his head. (Most convincing cartoons I've ever drawn.) She finally gave in. In 1948, I flew to Australia where we were married. Back in America we started our real-life "Family Circus" which was so enjoyable I wanted to share it with others. I launched the feature in 1960.

Through her help, understanding and love, Thel made it possible.

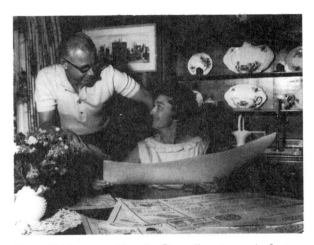

Since 1960 every "Family Circus" cartoon, before being mailed to the syndicate, has been carefully reviewed by Thel Keane, the real-life Heart of The Family Circus.